Table of Contents

Teacher Created Resources, Inc.
12621 Western Avenue
Garden Grove, CA 92841
www.teachercreated.com
ISBN: 978-1-4206-3716-8

Reprinted, 2019
Made in U.S.A.

Editor in Chief: *Karen Goldfluss, M.S. Ed.*

Creative Director: *Sarah M. Fournier*

Cover Design: *Denise Bauer*

Imaging: *Leonard P. Swierski*

Publisher: *Mary D. Smith, M.S. Ed.*

Teacher Created Resources

How to Use This Book

Standards Information (page 3)

Most teachers are required to write lesson plans each week, but in many school districts, lesson plans alone are no longer considered enough. A majority of school systems require teachers to address the standards that apply to their daily lessons. For background information about standards and a listing of national standards Internet websites, see page 3.

Substitute Teacher Information (pages 4 – 5)

Document all pertinent information on these pages. If you have a copy of the layout of your school, attach it to page 5. Otherwise, use the space provided on page 5 to sketch a diagram of the school building and grounds. Be sure to show important locations, such as the office, restrooms, faculty lounge, cafeteria, auditorium, and playground.

Student Roster (pages 6 – 7)

Use the roster to record information for each student. Having the roster in your lesson plan book provides you with quick and easy access to important data for both you and a substitute teacher.

Birthdays (page 8 – 9)

Use these pages to write students' names and birth dates. Recognize each special day with a birthday greeting.

Weekly Schedule (page 10)

If your schedule changes periodically, you may wish to duplicate this page before completing your current schedule. Attach new schedules throughout the year.

Monthly Planners (pages 11 – 16)

In addition to the daily lesson plan pages in this book, we have provided blank calendar pages for year-long planning. They can be used to note special plans, weekly/monthly meetings and appointments, and for other useful information throughout the year. You may wish to reproduce each month, add important information for the class, and then post the calendar months on a bulletin board or other display. Include special events, positive sayings, inspirational quotes, and friendly reminders on each calendar month.

Class Records (pages 17 – 76)

The class record section is designed to provide organized space for recording daily notations or grades for assignments, tests, attendance, tardies, participation, etc. Each page contains a five-week block of spaces so that a student's record for an entire quarter of ten weeks can be read on facing pages. Summary columns for recording total attendance, tardies, and grades appear on the right-hand facing page for each ten-week period.

Lesson Plans (pages 77 – 159)

Use the Daily Lesson Plans section to help you organize your lesson plans each week. There are enough weekly plan pages to cover a 40-week school year. At the top of the left-hand page, fill in the blank to indicate the week dates for which the plans are written. The first column may be used for notes. For special programs requiring more in-depth explanation of plans, reference the specific folder, notebook, guide, etc., to which the teacher should be directed. This is especially helpful to substitute teachers. On the top right-hand page of each week's lesson plans is a notable quotation. These quotations can serve as inspirational thoughts for teachers, as well as points of discussion and reflection for students.

Grading Chart (page 160)

A convenient chart for scoring students' work is provided at the back of this book. Use the chart as a quick reference when scoring 3 to 50 items of equal value. To use the chart, simply "connect" the row that matches the total number of items to be scored with the column indicating the number of incorrect items.

By following across the row and up the columns to the intersection point (number), you can determine the raw score. For example, if the total number of items on a given test is 35, and a student marked 5 incorrectly, his or her score would be 86%. The score is obtained by moving across row 35 and up column 5 to the point where they meet (86%).

Standards Information

What are standards, and why do we need them in education? A standard is a criteria or a guideline. Standards in education allow you to make a judgment about what a child should be able to do at a certain grade level. Once you've determined what he or she should be able to do, you can then help the child achieve educational goals.

Educational standards provide teachers with written expectations of what they need to teach during a school year. Standards are most often conveniently divided by grade level and subject matter. For example, a teacher in a fifth grade social studies class might be given a standard that states he or she is responsible for teaching students important historical figures from the Civil War era such as Abraham Lincoln, Frederick Douglass, and Robert E. Lee. The teacher uses the standard to know what to teach, but she then applies a benchmark to assess whether the students learned the standard. A benchmark might be anything from an oral report to a short quiz. Whatever the teacher decides to use to assess the learning, this benchmark helps her decide whether to stop and teach the standard again or whether to go on to the next standard listed in the guideline.

Background

Where do all these directions or guidelines come from, and how do you know which ones to use?

In the 1980's there was a move across the United States to standardize education in the core subject areas. It was a movement to ensure that students were headed in the same direction no matter who was giving the directions.

Individual states created frameworks or standards for different subjects and grade levels. Some of the standards overlapped from one grade level to the next. Some were divided into levels, such as standards that were just being introduced at a grade level, standards that were developing at a grade level, and standards that should be mastered at a grade level. But there was a push for something more; national standards for all states to use were also being created. These national standards provided a way for state education departments to be sure their students were meeting the same goals as students throughout the United States— in effect, creating a "standardization of standards" on a national level.

Getting Standards Information

With today's easy Internet access, a vast amount of information is available to those educators willing to take the time to look and learn. National standards for core subject areas can be accessed by researching some of the organizations listed below and by visiting their websites.

National Standards Websites

Common Core State Standards Initiative (CCSS) http://www.corestandards.org
National Council of Teachers of Mathematics (NCTM) http://www.nctm.org/standards/
National Council of Teachers of English (NCTE) http://www.ncte.org/standards
National Council for the Social Studies (NCSS) http://www.ncss.org/standards/
National Science Teachers Association (NSTA) http://www.nsta.org/publications/
National Council for Geographic Education (NCGE) http://www.ncge.org/resources
Next Generation Science Standards (NGSS) http://www.nextgenscience.org

School Schedule

- Class Begins ______
- Morning Recess ______
- Lunchtime ______
- Class Resumes ______
- Afternoon Recess ______
- Dismissal ______

Special Notes

______
______
______
______
______
______
______
______

Special Classes

Student ______
Class ______ Day ______ Time ______
Student ______
Class ______ Day ______ Time ______
Student ______
Class ______ Day ______ Time ______

Where to Find

- Class List ______
- School Layout ______
- Seating Chart ______
- Attendance Record ______
- Lesson Plans ______
- Teacher Manuals ______
- First Aid Kit ______
- Emergency Information ______
- Supplementary Activities ______
- Class Supplies–paper, pencils, etc. ______
- Referral forms and procedures ______

Special Needs Students

Student	Needs	Time and Place

Classroom Standards

- When finished with an assignment
- When and how to speak out in class
- Incentive Program
- Discipline
- Restroom Procedure

People Who Can Help

- Teacher/Room
- Dependable Students
- Principal
- Secretary
- Custodian
- Counselor
- Nurse

Map of Our School

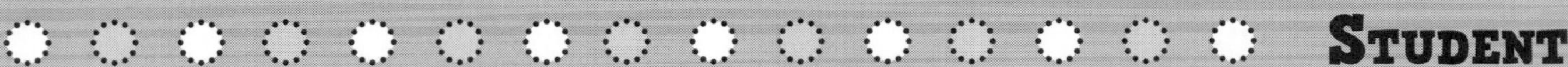

Student's Name	Parent's Name	Address
1.		
2		
3.		
4.		
5.		
6.		
7.		
8.		
9.		
10.		
11.		
12.		
13.		
14.		
15.		
16.		
17.		
18.		
19.		
20.		
21.		
22.		
23.		
24.		
25.		
26.		
27.		
28.		
29.		
30.		
31.		
32.		
33.		
34.		
35.		
36.		

Roster

Home & Work Phones	Birthday	Siblings	Notes

Birthdays

January	February	March

April	May	June

Birthdays

July	August	September

October	November	December

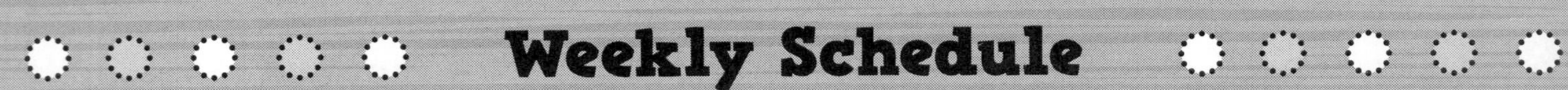

Time	Monday	Tuesday	Wednesday	Thursday	Friday

Notes

______________________________ Planner

Sunday	Monday	Tuesday	Wednesday	Thursday	Friday	Saturday

Notes

______________________________ Planner

Sunday	Monday	Tuesday	Wednesday	Thursday	Friday	Saturday

Notes	Planner						
	Sunday	Monday	Tuesday	Wednesday	Thursday	Friday	Saturday

Notes	Planner						
	Sunday	Monday	Tuesday	Wednesday	Thursday	Friday	Saturday

Notes

______________________ **Planner**

Sunday	Monday	Tuesday	Wednesday	Thursday	Friday	Saturday

Notes

______________________ **Planner**

Sunday	Monday	Tuesday	Wednesday	Thursday	Friday	Saturday

Notes	Planner						
	Sunday	Monday	Tuesday	Wednesday	Thursday	Friday	Saturday

Notes	Planner						
	Sunday	Monday	Tuesday	Wednesday	Thursday	Friday	Saturday

Notes	______ Planner						
	Sunday	Monday	Tuesday	Wednesday	Thursday	Friday	Saturday

Notes	______ Planner						
	Sunday	Monday	Tuesday	Wednesday	Thursday	Friday	Saturday

Planner

Notes

Sunday	Monday	Tuesday	Wednesday	Thursday	Friday	Saturday

Planner

Notes

Sunday	Monday	Tuesday	Wednesday	Thursday	Friday	Saturday

CLASS RECORDS

Subject ______ Time/Period ______	Assignments																									
Day		M	T	W	T	F	M	T	W	T	F	M	T	W	T	F	M	T	W	T	F	M	T	W	T	F
Name	Date→																									
	1																									
	2																									
	3																									
	4																									
	5																									
	6																									
	7																									
	8																									
	9																									
	10																									
	11																									
	12																									
	13																									
	14																									
	15																									
	16																									
	17																									
	18																									
	19																									
	20																									
	21																									
	22																									
	23																									
	24																									
	25																									
	26																									
	27																									
	28																									
	29																									
	30																									
	31																									
	32																									
	33																									
	34																									
	35																									
	36																									

M	T	W	T	F	M	T	W	T	F	M	T	W	T	F	M	T	W	T	F	M	T	W	T	F		Days Present	Days Absent	Tardies	Quarter Grade		
																									1						
																									2						
																									3						
																									4						
																									5						
																									6						
																									7						
																									8						
																									9						
																									10						
																									11						
																									12						
																									13						
																									14						
																									15						
																									16						
																									17						
																									18						
																									19						
																									20						
																									21						
																									22						
																									23						
																									24						
																									25						
																									26						
																									27						
																									28						
																									29						
																									30						
																									31						
																									32						
																									33						
																									34						
																									35						
																									36						

Subject

Time/Period

Assignments

Day		M	T	W	T	F	M	T	W	T	F	M	T	W	T	F	M	T	W	T	F	M	T	W	T	F
Name	Date→																									
	1																									
	2																									
	3																									
	4																									
	5																									
	6																									
	7																									
	8																									
	9																									
	10																									
	11																									
	12																									
	13																									
	14																									
	15																									
	16																									
	17																									
	18																									
	19																									
	20																									
	21																									
	22																									
	23																									
	24																									
	25																									
	26																									
	27																									
	28																									
	29																									
	30																									
	31																									
	32																									
	33																									
	34																									
	35																									
	36																									

M	T	W	T	F	M	T	W	T	F	M	T	W	T	F	M	T	W	T	F	M	T	W	T	F		Days Present	Days Absent	Tardies	Quarter Grade		
																									1						
																									2						
																									3						
																									4						
																									5						
																									6						
																									7						
																									8						
																									9						
																									10						
																									11						
																									12						
																									13						
																									14						
																									15						
																									16						
																									17						
																									18						
																									19						
																									20						
																									21						
																									22						
																									23						
																									24						
																									25						
																									26						
																									27						
																									28						
																									29						
																									30						
																									31						
																									32						
																									33						
																									34						
																									35						
																									36						

Subject / Time/Period	Assignments																									
Day		M	T	W	T	F	M	T	W	T	F	M	T	W	T	F	M	T	W	T	F	M	T	W	T	F
Name	Date→																									
	1																									
	2																									
	3																									
	4																									
	5																									
	6																									
	7																									
	8																									
	9																									
	10																									
	11																									
	12																									
	13																									
	14																									
	15																									
	16																									
	17																									
	18																									
	19																									
	20																									
	21																									
	22																									
	23																									
	24																									
	25																									
	26																									
	27																									
	28																									
	29																									
	30																									
	31																									
	32																									
	33																									
	34																									
	35																									
	36																									

M	T	W	T	F	M	T	W	T	F	M	T	W	T	F	M	T	W	T	F	M	T	W	T	F		Days Present	Days Absent	Tardies	Quarter Grade		
																									1						
																									2						
																									3						
																									4						
																									5						
																									6						
																									7						
																									8						
																									9						
																									10						
																									11						
																									12						
																									13						
																									14						
																									15						
																									16						
																									17						
																									18						
																									19						
																									20						
																									21						
																									22						
																									23						
																									24						
																									25						
																									26						
																									27						
																									28						
																									29						
																									30						
																									31						
																									32						
																									33						
																									34						
																									35						
																									36						

Subject ____________________

Time/Period ____________________

Assignments

Day	M	T	W	T	F	M	T	W	T	F	M	T	W	T	F	M	T	W	T	F	M	T	W	T	F
Name Date→																									
1																									
2																									
3																									
4																									
5																									
6																									
7																									
8																									
9																									
10																									
11																									
12																									
13																									
14																									
15																									
16																									
17																									
18																									
19																									
20																									
21																									
22																									
23																									
24																									
25																									
26																									
27																									
28																									
29																									
30																									
31																									
32																									
33																									
34																									
35																									
36																									

M	T	W	T	F	M	T	W	T	F	M	T	W	T	F	M	T	W	T	F	M	T	W	T	F		Days Present	Days Absent	Tardies	Quarter Grade		
																									1						
																									2						
																									3						
																									4						
																									5						
																									6						
																									7						
																									8						
																									9						
																									10						
																									11						
																									12						
																									13						
																									14						
																									15						
																									16						
																									17						
																									18						
																									19						
																									20						
																									21						
																									22						
																									23						
																									24						
																									25						
																									26						
																									27						
																									28						
																									29						
																									30						
																									31						
																									32						
																									33						
																									34						
																									35						
																									36						

Subject ____________ Time/Period ____________	Assignments																									
Day		M	T	W	T	F	M	T	W	T	F	M	T	W	T	F	M	T	W	T	F	M	T	W	T	F
Name	Date→																									
	1																									
	2																									
	3																									
	4																									
	5																									
	6																									
	7																									
	8																									
	9																									
	10																									
	11																									
	12																									
	13																									
	14																									
	15																									
	16																									
	17																									
	18																									
	19																									
	20																									
	21																									
	22																									
	23																									
	24																									
	25																									
	26																									
	27																									
	28																									
	29																									
	30																									
	31																									
	32																									
	33																									
	34																									
	35																									
	36																									

M	T	W	T	F	M	T	W	T	F	M	T	W	T	F	M	T	W	T	F	M	T	W	T	F		Days Present	Days Absent	Tardies	Quarter Grade		
																									1						
																									2						
																									3						
																									4						
																									5						
																									6						
																									7						
																									8						
																									9						
																									10						
																									11						
																									12						
																									13						
																									14						
																									15						
																									16						
																									17						
																									18						
																									19						
																									20						
																									21						
																									22						
																									23						
																									24						
																									25						
																									26						
																									27						
																									28						
																									29						
																									30						
																									31						
																									32						
																									33						
																									34						
																									35						
																									36						

Subject

Time/Period

Assignments

Day		M	T	W	T	F	M	T	W	T	F	M	T	W	T	F	M	T	W	T	F	M	T	W	T	F
Name	Date→																									
	1																									
	2																									
	3																									
	4																									
	5																									
	6																									
	7																									
	8																									
	9																									
	10																									
	11																									
	12																									
	13																									
	14																									
	15																									
	16																									
	17																									
	18																									
	19																									
	20																									
	21																									
	22																									
	23																									
	24																									
	25																									
	26																									
	27																									
	28																									
	29																									
	30																									
	31																									
	32																									
	33																									
	34																									
	35																									
	36																									

M	T	W	T	F	M	T	W	T	F	M	T	W	T	F	M	T	W	T	F	M	T	W	T	F		Days Present	Days Absent	Tardies	Quarter Grade		
																									1						
																									2						
																									3						
																									4						
																									5						
																									6						
																									7						
																									8						
																									9						
																									10						
																									11						
																									12						
																									13						
																									14						
																									15						
																									16						
																									17						
																									18						
																									19						
																									20						
																									21						
																									22						
																									23						
																									24						
																									25						
																									26						
																									27						
																									28						
																									29						
																									30						
																									31						
																									32						
																									33						
																									34						
																									35						
																									36						

Subject ____________________

Time/Period ____________________

Assignments

Day		M	T	W	T	F	M	T	W	T	F	M	T	W	T	F	M	T	W	T	F	M	T	W	T	F
Name	Date→																									
	1																									
	2																									
	3																									
	4																									
	5																									
	6																									
	7																									
	8																									
	9																									
	10																									
	11																									
	12																									
	13																									
	14																									
	15																									
	16																									
	17																									
	18																									
	19																									
	20																									
	21																									
	22																									
	23																									
	24																									
	25																									
	26																									
	27																									
	28																									
	29																									
	30																									
	31																									
	32																									
	33																									
	34																									
	35																									
	36																									

M	T	W	T	F	M	T	W	T	F	M	T	W	T	F	M	T	W	T	F	M	T	W	T	F		Days Present	Days Absent	Tardies	Quarter Grade		
																									1						
																									2						
																									3						
																									4						
																									5						
																									6						
																									7						
																									8						
																									9						
																									10						
																									11						
																									12						
																									13						
																									14						
																									15						
																									16						
																									17						
																									18						
																									19						
																									20						
																									21						
																									22						
																									23						
																									24						
																									25						
																									26						
																									27						
																									28						
																									29						
																									30						
																									31						
																									32						
																									33						
																									34						
																									35						
																									36						

Subject ____ Time/Period ____	Assignments																								
Day		M	T	W	T	F	M	T	W	T	F	M	T	W	T	F	M	T	W	T	F	M	T	W	T	F
Name	Date→																									
	1																									
	2																									
	3																									
	4																									
	5																									
	6																									
	7																									
	8																									
	9																									
	10																									
	11																									
	12																									
	13																									
	14																									
	15																									
	16																									
	17																									
	18																									
	19																									
	20																									
	21																									
	22																									
	23																									
	24																									
	25																									
	26																									
	27																									
	28																									
	29																									
	30																									
	31																									
	32																									
	33																									
	34																									
	35																									
	36																									

M	T	W	T	F	M	T	W	T	F	M	T	W	T	F	M	T	W	T	F	M	T	W	T	F		Days Present	Days Absent	Tardies	Quarter Grade		
																									1						
																									2						
																									3						
																									4						
																									5						
																									6						
																									7						
																									8						
																									9						
																									10						
																									11						
																									12						
																									13						
																									14						
																									15						
																									16						
																									17						
																									18						
																									19						
																									20						
																									21						
																									22						
																									23						
																									24						
																									25						
																									26						
																									27						
																									28						
																									29						
																									30						
																									31						
																									32						
																									33						
																									34						
																									35						
																									36						

Subject

Time/Period

Assignments																									
Day	M	T	W	T	F	M	T	W	T	F	M	T	W	T	F	M	T	W	T	F	M	T	W	T	F
Name Date→																									
1																									
2																									
3																									
4																									
5																									
6																									
7																									
8																									
9																									
10																									
11																									
12																									
13																									
14																									
15																									
16																									
17																									
18																									
19																									
20																									
21																									
22																									
23																									
24																									
25																									
26																									
27																									
28																									
29																									
30																									
31																									
32																									
33																									
34																									
35																									
36																									

M	T	W	T	F	M	T	W	T	F	M	T	W	T	F	M	T	W	T	F	M	T	W	T	F		Days Present	Days Absent	Tardies	Quarter Grade		
																									1						
																									2						
																									3						
																									4						
																									5						
																									6						
																									7						
																									8						
																									9						
																									10						
																									11						
																									12						
																									13						
																									14						
																									15						
																									16						
																									17						
																									18						
																									19						
																									20						
																									21						
																									22						
																									23						
																									24						
																									25						
																									26						
																									27						
																									28						
																									29						
																									30						
																									31						
																									32						
																									33						
																									34						
																									35						
																									36						

Subject ____________________

Time/Period ____________________

Day	M	T	W	T	F	M	T	W	T	F	M	T	W	T	F	M	T	W	T	F	M	T	W	T	F
Assignments																									
Name Date→																									
1																									
2																									
3																									
4																									
5																									
6																									
7																									
8																									
9																									
10																									
11																									
12																									
13																									
14																									
15																									
16																									
17																									
18																									
19																									
20																									
21																									
22																									
23																									
24																									
25																									
26																									
27																									
28																									
29																									
30																									
31																									
32																									
33																									
34																									
35																									
36																									

M	T	W	T	F	M	T	W	T	F	M	T	W	T	F	M	T	W	T	F	M	T	W	T	F		Days Present	Days Absent	Tardies	Quarter Grade		
																									1						
																									2						
																									3						
																									4						
																									5						
																									6						
																									7						
																									8						
																									9						
																									10						
																									11						
																									12						
																									13						
																									14						
																									15						
																									16						
																									17						
																									18						
																									19						
																									20						
																									21						
																									22						
																									23						
																									24						
																									25						
																									26						
																									27						
																									28						
																									29						
																									30						
																									31						
																									32						
																									33						
																									34						
																									35						
																									36						

Subject ________ Time/Period ________	Assignments																									
Day		M	T	W	T	F	M	T	W	T	F	M	T	W	T	F	M	T	W	T	F	M	T	W	T	F
Name	Date→																									
	1																									
	2																									
	3																									
	4																									
	5																									
	6																									
	7																									
	8																									
	9																									
	10																									
	11																									
	12																									
	13																									
	14																									
	15																									
	16																									
	17																									
	18																									
	19																									
	20																									
	21																									
	22																									
	23																									
	24																									
	25																									
	26																									
	27																									
	28																									
	29																									
	30																									
	31																									
	32																									
	33																									
	34																									
	35																									
	36																									

M	T	W	T	F	M	T	W	T	F	M	T	W	T	F	M	T	W	T	F	M	T	W	T	F		Days Present	Days Absent	Tardies	Quarter Grade		
																									1						
																									2						
																									3						
																									4						
																									5						
																									6						
																									7						
																									8						
																									9						
																									10						
																									11						
																									12						
																									13						
																									14						
																									15						
																									16						
																									17						
																									18						
																									19						
																									20						
																									21						
																									22						
																									23						
																									24						
																									25						
																									26						
																									27						
																									28						
																									29						
																									30						
																									31						
																									32						
																									33						
																									34						
																									35						
																									36						

Subject ____________________

Time/Period ____________________

Assignments																										
Day		M	T	W	T	F	M	T	W	T	F	M	T	W	T	F	M	T	W	T	F	M	T	W	T	F
Name	Date→																									
	1																									
	2																									
	3																									
	4																									
	5																									
	6																									
	7																									
	8																									
	9																									
	10																									
	11																									
	12																									
	13																									
	14																									
	15																									
	16																									
	17																									
	18																									
	19																									
	20																									
	21																									
	22																									
	23																									
	24																									
	25																									
	26																									
	27																									
	28																									
	29																									
	30																									
	31																									
	32																									
	33																									
	34																									
	35																									
	36																									

M	T	W	T	F	M	T	W	T	F	M	T	W	T	F	M	T	W	T	F	M	T	W	T	F		Days Present	Days Absent	Tardies	Quarter Grade		
																									1						
																									2						
																									3						
																									4						
																									5						
																									6						
																									7						
																									8						
																									9						
																									10						
																									11						
																									12						
																									13						
																									14						
																									15						
																									16						
																									17						
																									18						
																									19						
																									20						
																									21						
																									22						
																									23						
																									24						
																									25						
																									26						
																									27						
																									28						
																									29						
																									30						
																									31						
																									32						
																									33						
																									34						
																									35						
																									36						

Subject ______________

Time/Period ______________

Assignments

Day	M	T	W	T	F	M	T	W	T	F	M	T	W	T	F	M	T	W	T	F	M	T	W	T	F
Name Date→																									
1																									
2																									
3																									
4																									
5																									
6																									
7																									
8																									
9																									
10																									
11																									
12																									
13																									
14																									
15																									
16																									
17																									
18																									
19																									
20																									
21																									
22																									
23																									
24																									
25																									
26																									
27																									
28																									
29																									
30																									
31																									
32																									
33																									
34																									
35																									
36																									

M	T	W	T	F	M	T	W	T	F	M	T	W	T	F	M	T	W	T	F	M	T	W	T	F		Days Present	Days Absent	Tardies	Quarter Grade		
																									1						
																									2						
																									3						
																									4						
																									5						
																									6						
																									7						
																									8						
																									9						
																									10						
																									11						
																									12						
																									13						
																									14						
																									15						
																									16						
																									17						
																									18						
																									19						
																									20						
																									21						
																									22						
																									23						
																									24						
																									25						
																									26						
																									27						
																									28						
																									29						
																									30						
																									31						
																									32						
																									33						
																									34						
																									35						
																									36						

Subject ______________

Time/Period ______________

Assignments

Day		M	T	W	T	F	M	T	W	T	F	M	T	W	T	F	M	T	W	T	F	M	T	W	T	F
Name	Date→																									
	1																									
	2																									
	3																									
	4																									
	5																									
	6																									
	7																									
	8																									
	9																									
	10																									
	11																									
	12																									
	13																									
	14																									
	15																									
	16																									
	17																									
	18																									
	19																									
	20																									
	21																									
	22																									
	23																									
	24																									
	25																									
	26																									
	27																									
	28																									
	29																									
	30																									
	31																									
	32																									
	33																									
	34																									
	35																									
	36																									

M	T	W	T	F	M	T	W	T	F	M	T	W	T	F	M	T	W	T	F	M	T	W	T	F		Days Present	Days Absent	Tardies	Quarter Grade		
																									1						
																									2						
																									3						
																									4						
																									5						
																									6						
																									7						
																									8						
																									9						
																									10						
																									11						
																									12						
																									13						
																									14						
																									15						
																									16						
																									17						
																									18						
																									19						
																									20						
																									21						
																									22						
																									23						
																									24						
																									25						
																									26						
																									27						
																									28						
																									29						
																									30						
																									31						
																									32						
																									33						
																									34						
																									35						
																									36						

Subject ____________________

Time/Period ____________________

Assignments

Day		M	T	W	T	F	M	T	W	T	F	M	T	W	T	F	M	T	W	T	F	M	T	W	T	F
Name	Date→																									
	1																									
	2																									
	3																									
	4																									
	5																									
	6																									
	7																									
	8																									
	9																									
	10																									
	11																									
	12																									
	13																									
	14																									
	15																									
	16																									
	17																									
	18																									
	19																									
	20																									
	21																									
	22																									
	23																									
	24																									
	25																									
	26																									
	27																									
	28																									
	29																									
	30																									
	31																									
	32																									
	33																									
	34																									
	35																									
	36																									

M	T	W	T	F	M	T	W	T	F	M	T	W	T	F	M	T	W	T	F	M	T	W	T	F		Days Present	Days Absent	Tardies	Quarter Grade		
																									1						
																									2						
																									3						
																									4						
																									5						
																									6						
																									7						
																									8						
																									9						
																									10						
																									11						
																									12						
																									13						
																									14						
																									15						
																									16						
																									17						
																									18						
																									19						
																									20						
																									21						
																									22						
																									23						
																									24						
																									25						
																									26						
																									27						
																									28						
																									29						
																									30						
																									31						
																									32						
																									33						
																									34						
																									35						
																									36						

Subject

Time/Period

Assignments

Day		M	T	W	T	F	M	T	W	T	F	M	T	W	T	F	M	T	W	T	F	M	T	W	T	F
Name	Date→																									
	1																									
	2																									
	3																									
	4																									
	5																									
	6																									
	7																									
	8																									
	9																									
	10																									
	11																									
	12																									
	13																									
	14																									
	15																									
	16																									
	17																									
	18																									
	19																									
	20																									
	21																									
	22																									
	23																									
	24																									
	25																									
	26																									
	27																									
	28																									
	29																									
	30																									
	31																									
	32																									
	33																									
	34																									
	35																									
	36																									

M	T	W	T	F	M	T	W	T	F	M	T	W	T	F	M	T	W	T	F	M	T	W	T	F		Days Present	Days Absent	Tardies	Quarter Grade		
																									1						
																									2						
																									3						
																									4						
																									5						
																									6						
																									7						
																									8						
																									9						
																									10						
																									11						
																									12						
																									13						
																									14						
																									15						
																									16						
																									17						
																									18						
																									19						
																									20						
																									21						
																									22						
																									23						
																									24						
																									25						
																									26						
																									27						
																									28						
																									29						
																									30						
																									31						
																									32						
																									33						
																									34						
																									35						
																									36						

Subject ______________________

Time/Period ______________________

	Assignments																									
Day		M	T	W	T	F	M	T	W	T	F	M	T	W	T	F	M	T	W	T	F	M	T	W	T	F
Name	Date→																									
	1																									
	2																									
	3																									
	4																									
	5																									
	6																									
	7																									
	8																									
	9																									
	10																									
	11																									
	12																									
	13																									
	14																									
	15																									
	16																									
	17																									
	18																									
	19																									
	20																									
	21																									
	22																									
	23																									
	24																									
	25																									
	26																									
	27																									
	28																									
	29																									
	30																									
	31																									
	32																									
	33																									
	34																									
	35																									
	36																									

M	T	W	T	F	M	T	W	T	F	M	T	W	T	F	M	T	W	T	F	M	T	W	T	F		Days Present	Days Absent	Tardies	Quarter Grade		
																									1						
																									2						
																									3						
																									4						
																									5						
																									6						
																									7						
																									8						
																									9						
																									10						
																									11						
																									12						
																									13						
																									14						
																									15						
																									16						
																									17						
																									18						
																									19						
																									20						
																									21						
																									22						
																									23						
																									24						
																									25						
																									26						
																									27						
																									28						
																									29						
																									30						
																									31						
																									32						
																									33						
																									34						
																									35						
																									36						

Subject

Time/Period

Assignments

Day		M	T	W	T	F	M	T	W	T	F	M	T	W	T	F	M	T	W	T	F	M	T	W	T	F
Name	Date→																									
	1																									
	2																									
	3																									
	4																									
	5																									
	6																									
	7																									
	8																									
	9																									
	10																									
	11																									
	12																									
	13																									
	14																									
	15																									
	16																									
	17																									
	18																									
	19																									
	20																									
	21																									
	22																									
	23																									
	24																									
	25																									
	26																									
	27																									
	28																									
	29																									
	30																									
	31																									
	32																									
	33																									
	34																									
	35																									
	36																									

M	T	W	T	F	M	T	W	T	F	M	T	W	T	F	M	T	W	T	F	M	T	W	T	F		Days Present	Days Absent	Tardies	Quarter Grade		
																									1						
																									2						
																									3						
																									4						
																									5						
																									6						
																									7						
																									8						
																									9						
																									10						
																									11						
																									12						
																									13						
																									14						
																									15						
																									16						
																									17						
																									18						
																									19						
																									20						
																									21						
																									22						
																									23						
																									24						
																									25						
																									26						
																									27						
																									28						
																									29						
																									30						
																									31						
																									32						
																									33						
																									34						
																									35						
																									36						

Subject ____________________

Time/Period ____________________

Assignments

Day	M	T	W	T	F	M	T	W	T	F	M	T	W	T	F	M	T	W	T	F	M	T	W	T	F
Name Date→																									
1																									
2																									
3																									
4																									
5																									
6																									
7																									
8																									
9																									
10																									
11																									
12																									
13																									
14																									
15																									
16																									
17																									
18																									
19																									
20																									
21																									
22																									
23																									
24																									
25																									
26																									
27																									
28																									
29																									
30																									
31																									
32																									
33																									
34																									
35																									
36																									

M	T	W	T	F	M	T	W	T	F	M	T	W	T	F	M	T	W	T	F	M	T	W	T	F		Days Present	Days Absent	Tardies	Quarter Grade		
																									1						
																									2						
																									3						
																									4						
																									5						
																									6						
																									7						
																									8						
																									9						
																									10						
																									11						
																									12						
																									13						
																									14						
																									15						
																									16						
																									17						
																									18						
																									19						
																									20						
																									21						
																									22						
																									23						
																									24						
																									25						
																									26						
																									27						
																									28						
																									29						
																									30						
																									31						
																									32						
																									33						
																									34						
																									35						
																									36						

Subject ____________________

Time/Period ____________________

Assignments

Day	M	T	W	T	F	M	T	W	T	F	M	T	W	T	F	M	T	W	T	F	M	T	W	T	F
Name Date→																									
1																									
2																									
3																									
4																									
5																									
6																									
7																									
8																									
9																									
10																									
11																									
12																									
13																									
14																									
15																									
16																									
17																									
18																									
19																									
20																									
21																									
22																									
23																									
24																									
25																									
26																									
27																									
28																									
29																									
30																									
31																									
32																									
33																									
34																									
35																									
36																									

M	T	W	T	F	M	T	W	T	F	M	T	W	T	F	M	T	W	T	F	M	T	W	T	F		Days Present	Days Absent	Tardies	Quarter Grade		
																									1						
																									2						
																									3						
																									4						
																									5						
																									6						
																									7						
																									8						
																									9						
																									10						
																									11						
																									12						
																									13						
																									14						
																									15						
																									16						
																									17						
																									18						
																									19						
																									20						
																									21						
																									22						
																									23						
																									24						
																									25						
																									26						
																									27						
																									28						
																									29						
																									30						
																									31						
																									32						
																									33						
																									34						
																									35						
																									36						

Subject ____________________

Time/Period ____________________

Day		M	T	W	T	F	M	T	W	T	F	M	T	W	T	F	M	T	W	T	F	M	T	W	T	F
Assignments																										
Name	Date→																									
	1																									
	2																									
	3																									
	4																									
	5																									
	6																									
	7																									
	8																									
	9																									
	10																									
	11																									
	12																									
	13																									
	14																									
	15																									
	16																									
	17																									
	18																									
	19																									
	20																									
	21																									
	22																									
	23																									
	24																									
	25																									
	26																									
	27																									
	28																									
	29																									
	30																									
	31																									
	32																									
	33																									
	34																									
	35																									
	36																									

M	T	W	T	F	M	T	W	T	F	M	T	W	T	F	M	T	W	T	F	M	T	W	T	F		Days Present	Days Absent	Tardies	Quarter Grade		
																									1						
																									2						
																									3						
																									4						
																									5						
																									6						
																									7						
																									8						
																									9						
																									10						
																									11						
																									12						
																									13						
																									14						
																									15						
																									16						
																									17						
																									18						
																									19						
																									20						
																									21						
																									22						
																									23						
																									24						
																									25						
																									26						
																									27						
																									28						
																									29						
																									30						
																									31						
																									32						
																									33						
																									34						
																									35						
																									36						

Subject ______________________

Time/Period ______________________

Day		M	T	W	T	F	M	T	W	T	F	M	T	W	T	F	M	T	W	T	F	M	T	W	T	F
Assignments																										
Name	Date→																									
	1																									
	2																									
	3																									
	4																									
	5																									
	6																									
	7																									
	8																									
	9																									
	10																									
	11																									
	12																									
	13																									
	14																									
	15																									
	16																									
	17																									
	18																									
	19																									
	20																									
	21																									
	22																									
	23																									
	24																									
	25																									
	26																									
	27																									
	28																									
	29																									
	30																									
	31																									
	32																									
	33																									
	34																									
	35																									
	36																									

M	T	W	T	F	M	T	W	T	F	M	T	W	T	F	M	T	W	T	F	M	T	W	T	F		Days Present	Days Absent	Tardies	Quarter Grade		
																									1						
																									2						
																									3						
																									4						
																									5						
																									6						
																									7						
																									8						
																									9						
																									10						
																									11						
																									12						
																									13						
																									14						
																									15						
																									16						
																									17						
																									18						
																									19						
																									20						
																									21						
																									22						
																									23						
																									24						
																									25						
																									26						
																									27						
																									28						
																									29						
																									30						
																									31						
																									32						
																									33						
																									34						
																									35						
																									36						

Subject ______________________

Time/Period ______________________

Assignments

Day	M	T	W	T	F	M	T	W	T	F	M	T	W	T	F	M	T	W	T	F	M	T	W	T	F
Name Date→																									
1																									
2																									
3																									
4																									
5																									
6																									
7																									
8																									
9																									
10																									
11																									
12																									
13																									
14																									
15																									
16																									
17																									
18																									
19																									
20																									
21																									
22																									
23																									
24																									
25																									
26																									
27																									
28																									
29																									
30																									
31																									
32																									
33																									
34																									
35																									
36																									

M	T	W	T	F	M	T	W	T	F	M	T	W	T	F	M	T	W	T	F	M	T	W	T	F		Days Present	Days Absent	Tardies	Quarter Grade		
																									1						
																									2						
																									3						
																									4						
																									5						
																									6						
																									7						
																									8						
																									9						
																									10						
																									11						
																									12						
																									13						
																									14						
																									15						
																									16						
																									17						
																									18						
																									19						
																									20						
																									21						
																									22						
																									23						
																									24						
																									25						
																									26						
																									27						
																									28						
																									29						
																									30						
																									31						
																									32						
																									33						
																									34						
																									35						
																									36						

Subject

Time/Period

Assignments

Day		M	T	W	T	F	M	T	W	T	F	M	T	W	T	F	M	T	W	T	F	M	T	W	T	F
Name	Date→																									
	1																									
	2																									
	3																									
	4																									
	5																									
	6																									
	7																									
	8																									
	9																									
	10																									
	11																									
	12																									
	13																									
	14																									
	15																									
	16																									
	17																									
	18																									
	19																									
	20																									
	21																									
	22																									
	23																									
	24																									
	25																									
	26																									
	27																									
	28																									
	29																									
	30																									
	31																									
	32																									
	33																									
	34																									
	35																									
	36																									

M	T	W	T	F	M	T	W	T	F	M	T	W	T	F	M	T	W	T	F	M	T	W	T	F		Days Present	Days Absent	Tardies	Quarter Grade		
																									1						
																									2						
																									3						
																									4						
																									5						
																									6						
																									7						
																									8						
																									9						
																									10						
																									11						
																									12						
																									13						
																									14						
																									15						
																									16						
																									17						
																									18						
																									19						
																									20						
																									21						
																									22						
																									23						
																									24						
																									25						
																									26						
																									27						
																									28						
																									29						
																									30						
																									31						
																									32						
																									33						
																									34						
																									35						
																									36						

Subject ____________________

Time/Period ____________________

Assignments

Day	M	T	W	T	F	M	T	W	T	F	M	T	W	T	F	M	T	W	T	F	M	T	W	T	F
Name Date→																									
1																									
2																									
3																									
4																									
5																									
6																									
7																									
8																									
9																									
10																									
11																									
12																									
13																									
14																									
15																									
16																									
17																									
18																									
19																									
20																									
21																									
22																									
23																									
24																									
25																									
26																									
27																									
28																									
29																									
30																									
31																									
32																									
33																									
34																									
35																									
36																									

M	T	W	T	F	M	T	W	T	F	M	T	W	T	F	M	T	W	T	F	M	T	W	T	F		Days Present	Days Absent	Tardies	Quarter Grade		
																									1						
																									2						
																									3						
																									4						
																									5						
																									6						
																									7						
																									8						
																									9						
																									10						
																									11						
																									12						
																									13						
																									14						
																									15						
																									16						
																									17						
																									18						
																									19						
																									20						
																									21						
																									22						
																									23						
																									24						
																									25						
																									26						
																									27						
																									28						
																									29						
																									30						
																									31						
																									32						
																									33						
																									34						
																									35						
																									36						

Subject

Time/Period

Assignments

Day		M	T	W	T	F	M	T	W	T	F	M	T	W	T	F	M	T	W	T	F	M	T	W	T	F
Name	Date→																									
	1																									
	2																									
	3																									
	4																									
	5																									
	6																									
	7																									
	8																									
	9																									
	10																									
	11																									
	12																									
	13																									
	14																									
	15																									
	16																									
	17																									
	18																									
	19																									
	20																									
	21																									
	22																									
	23																									
	24																									
	25																									
	26																									
	27																									
	28																									
	29																									
	30																									
	31																									
	32																									
	33																									
	34																									
	35																									
	36																									

M	T	W	T	F	M	T	W	T	F	M	T	W	T	F	M	T	W	T	F	M	T	W	T	F		Days Present	Days Absent	Tardies	Quarter Grade		
																									1						
																									2						
																									3						
																									4						
																									5						
																									6						
																									7						
																									8						
																									9						
																									10						
																									11						
																									12						
																									13						
																									14						
																									15						
																									16						
																									17						
																									18						
																									19						
																									20						
																									21						
																									22						
																									23						
																									24						
																									25						
																									26						
																									27						
																									28						
																									29						
																									30						
																									31						
																									32						
																									33						
																									34						
																									35						
																									36						

Subject ______________________

Time/Period ______________________

Day	M	T	W	T	F	M	T	W	T	F	M	T	W	T	F	M	T	W	T	F	M	T	W	T	F
Assignments																									
Name Date→																									
1																									
2																									
3																									
4																									
5																									
6																									
7																									
8																									
9																									
10																									
11																									
12																									
13																									
14																									
15																									
16																									
17																									
18																									
19																									
20																									
21																									
22																									
23																									
24																									
25																									
26																									
27																									
28																									
29																									
30																									
31																									
32																									
33																									
34																									
35																									
36																									

M	T	W	T	F	M	T	W	T	F	M	T	W	T	F	M	T	W	T	F	M	T	W	T	F		Days Present	Days Absent	Tardies	Quarter Grade		
																									1						
																									2						
																									3						
																									4						
																									5						
																									6						
																									7						
																									8						
																									9						
																									10						
																									11						
																									12						
																									13						
																									14						
																									15						
																									16						
																									17						
																									18						
																									19						
																									20						
																									21						
																									22						
																									23						
																									24						
																									25						
																									26						
																									27						
																									28						
																									29						
																									30						
																									31						
																									32						
																									33						
																									34						
																									35						
																									36						

Subject

Time/Period

Assignments

Day		M	T	W	T	F	M	T	W	T	F	M	T	W	T	F	M	T	W	T	F	M	T	W	T	F
Name	Date→																									
	1																									
	2																									
	3																									
	4																									
	5																									
	6																									
	7																									
	8																									
	9																									
	10																									
	11																									
	12																									
	13																									
	14																									
	15																									
	16																									
	17																									
	18																									
	19																									
	20																									
	21																									
	22																									
	23																									
	24																									
	25																									
	26																									
	27																									
	28																									
	29																									
	30																									
	31																									
	32																									
	33																									
	34																									
	35																									
	36																									

M	T	W	T	F	M	T	W	T	F	M	T	W	T	F	M	T	W	T	F	M	T	W	T	F		Days Present	Days Absent	Tardies	Quarter Grade		
																									1						
																									2						
																									3						
																									4						
																									5						
																									6						
																									7						
																									8						
																									9						
																									10						
																									11						
																									12						
																									13						
																									14						
																									15						
																									16						
																									17						
																									18						
																									19						
																									20						
																									21						
																									22						
																									23						
																									24						
																									25						
																									26						
																									27						
																									28						
																									29						
																									30						
																									31						
																									32						
																									33						
																									34						
																									35						
																									36						

Subject ______________________

Time/Period ______________________

	Assignments																									
Day		M	T	W	T	F	M	T	W	T	F	M	T	W	T	F	M	T	W	T	F	M	T	W	T	F
Name	Date→																									
	1																									
	2																									
	3																									
	4																									
	5																									
	6																									
	7																									
	8																									
	9																									
	10																									
	11																									
	12																									
	13																									
	14																									
	15																									
	16																									
	17																									
	18																									
	19																									
	20																									
	21																									
	22																									
	23																									
	24																									
	25																									
	26																									
	27																									
	28																									
	29																									
	30																									
	31																									
	32																									
	33																									
	34																									
	35																									
	36																									

M	T	W	T	F	M	T	W	T	F	M	T	W	T	F	M	T	W	T	F	M	T	W	T	F		Days Present	Days Absent	Tardies	Quarter Grade		
																									1						
																									2						
																									3						
																									4						
																									5						
																									6						
																									7						
																									8						
																									9						
																									10						
																									11						
																									12						
																									13						
																									14						
																									15						
																									16						
																									17						
																									18						
																									19						
																									20						
																									21						
																									22						
																									23						
																									24						
																									25						
																									26						
																									27						
																									28						
																									29						
																									30						
																									31						
																									32						
																									33						
																									34						
																									35						
																									36						

Notes

LESSON PLANS

Week of

NOTES	MONDAY	TUESDAY

WEDNESDAY	THURSDAY	FRIDAY

Week of

NOTES	MONDAY	TUESDAY

Whether you think you can or think you can't, you are right. — Henry Ford

WEDNESDAY	THURSDAY	FRIDAY

Week of

NOTES	MONDAY	TUESDAY

WEDNESDAY	THURSDAY	FRIDAY

Week of

NOTES	MONDAY	TUESDAY

Failure is a detour, not a dead-end street. — Zig Ziglar

WEDNESDAY	THURSDAY	FRIDAY

Week of

NOTES	MONDAY	TUESDAY

No act of kindness, no matter how small, is ever wasted. — Aesop

WEDNESDAY	THURSDAY	FRIDAY

Week of

NOTES	MONDAY	TUESDAY

WEDNESDAY	THURSDAY	FRIDAY

Week of

NOTES	MONDAY	TUESDAY

WEDNESDAY	THURSDAY	FRIDAY

Week of

NOTES	MONDAY	TUESDAY

WEDNESDAY	THURSDAY	FRIDAY

Week of

NOTES	MONDAY	TUESDAY

People are about as happy as they make up their minds to be. — Abraham Lincoln

WEDNESDAY	THURSDAY	FRIDAY

Week of

NOTES	MONDAY	TUESDAY

Life is a succession of moments. To live each one is to succeed. — *Corita Kent*

WEDNESDAY	THURSDAY	FRIDAY

Week of

NOTES	MONDAY	TUESDAY

WEDNESDAY	THURSDAY	FRIDAY

Week of

NOTES	MONDAY	TUESDAY

We plant trees not for ourselves, but for future generations. — Caecilius Statius

WEDNESDAY	THURSDAY	FRIDAY

Week of

NOTES	MONDAY	TUESDAY

The world is but a canvas to the imagination. — *Henry David Thoreau*

WEDNESDAY	THURSDAY	FRIDAY

Week of

NOTES	MONDAY	TUESDAY

WEDNESDAY	THURSDAY	FRIDAY

Week of

NOTES	MONDAY	TUESDAY

WEDNESDAY	THURSDAY	FRIDAY

Week of

NOTES	MONDAY	TUESDAY

To accomplish great things, we must dream as well as act. — Anatole France

WEDNESDAY	THURSDAY	FRIDAY

Week of

NOTES	MONDAY	TUESDAY

Attitude is a little thing that makes a big difference. — *Winston Churchill*

WEDNESDAY	THURSDAY	FRIDAY

Week of

NOTES	MONDAY	TUESDAY

All things are difficult before they are easy. — English Proverb

WEDNESDAY	THURSDAY	FRIDAY

Week of

NOTES	MONDAY	TUESDAY

WEDNESDAY	THURSDAY	FRIDAY

Week of

NOTES	MONDAY	TUESDAY

WEDNESDAY	THURSDAY	FRIDAY

Week of

NOTES	MONDAY	TUESDAY

WEDNESDAY	THURSDAY	FRIDAY

Week of

NOTES	MONDAY	TUESDAY

WEDNESDAY	THURSDAY	FRIDAY

Week of

NOTES	MONDAY	TUESDAY

A good head and a good heart are always a formidable combination. — Nelson Mandela

WEDNESDAY	THURSDAY	FRIDAY

Week of

NOTES	MONDAY	TUESDAY

WEDNESDAY	THURSDAY	FRIDAY

Week of

NOTES	MONDAY	TUESDAY

WEDNESDAY	THURSDAY	FRIDAY

Week of

NOTES	MONDAY	TUESDAY

WEDNESDAY	THURSDAY	FRIDAY

Week of

NOTES	MONDAY	TUESDAY

With the new day comes new strength and new thoughts. — Eleanor Roosevelt

WEDNESDAY	THURSDAY	FRIDAY

Week of

NOTES	MONDAY	TUESDAY

Strength lies in differences, not in similarities. — Stephen Covey

WEDNESDAY	THURSDAY	FRIDAY

Week of

NOTES	MONDAY	TUESDAY

WEDNESDAY	THURSDAY	FRIDAY

Week of

NOTES	MONDAY	TUESDAY

WEDNESDAY	THURSDAY	FRIDAY

Week of

NOTES	MONDAY	TUESDAY

A leader is one who knows the way, goes the way, and shows the way. —John C. Maxwell

WEDNESDAY	THURSDAY	FRIDAY

Week of

NOTES	MONDAY	TUESDAY

WEDNESDAY	THURSDAY	FRIDAY

Week of

NOTES	MONDAY	TUESDAY

WEDNESDAY	THURSDAY	FRIDAY

Week of

NOTES	MONDAY	TUESDAY

Education is not the filling of a pail, but the lighting of a fire. — William Butler Yeats

WEDNESDAY	THURSDAY	FRIDAY

Week of

NOTES	MONDAY	TUESDAY

WEDNESDAY	THURSDAY	FRIDAY

Week of

NOTES	MONDAY	TUESDAY

The art of teaching is the art of assisting discovery. — Mark Van Doren

WEDNESDAY	THURSDAY	FRIDAY

Week of

NOTES	MONDAY	TUESDAY

WEDNESDAY	THURSDAY	FRIDAY

Week of

NOTES	MONDAY	TUESDAY

Learning is a treasure that will follow its owner everywhere. — Chinese Proverb

WEDNESDAY	THURSDAY	FRIDAY

Week of

NOTES	MONDAY	TUESDAY

The best way to know life is to love many things. — Vincent Van Gogh

WEDNESDAY	THURSDAY	FRIDAY

Week of

NOTES	MONDAY	TUESDAY

One's work may be finished someday, but one's education never. — *Alexandre Dumas*

WEDNESDAY	THURSDAY	FRIDAY

Week of

NOTES	MONDAY	TUESDAY

It is a rough road that leads to the heights of greatness. — Seneca

WEDNESDAY	THURSDAY	FRIDAY

GRADING CHART

Total Number of Items	1	2	3	4	5	6	7	8	9	10	11	12	13	14	15	16	17	18	19	20	21	22	23	24	25	26	27	28	29	30
50	98	96	94	92	90	88	86	84	82	80	78	76	74	72	70	68	66	64	62	60	58	56	54	52	50	48	46	44	42	40
49	98	96	94	92	90	88	86	84	82	80	78	76	73	71	69	67	65	63	61	59	57	55	53	51	49	47	45	43	41	39
48	98	96	94	92	90	88	85	83	81	79	77	75	73	71	69	67	65	63	60	58	56	54	52	50	48	46	44	42	40	38
47	98	96	94	91	89	87	85	83	81	79	77	74	72	70	68	66	64	62	60	57	55	53	51	49	47	45	43	40	38	36
46	98	96	93	91	89	87	85	81	80	78	76	74	72	70	67	65	63	61	59	57	54	52	50	48	46	43	41	39	37	35
45	98	95	93	91	89	87	84	82	80	78	76	73	71	69	67	64	62	60	58	56	53	51	49	47	44	42	40	38	36	33
44	98	95	93	91	89	86	84	82	80	77	75	73	70	68	66	64	61	59	57	55	52	50	48	45	43	41	39	36	34	32
43	98	95	93	91	88	86	84	81	79	77	74	72	70	67	65	63	60	58	56	53	51	49	47	44	42	40	37	35	33	30
42	98	95	93	90	88	86	83	81	79	76	74	71	69	67	64	62	60	57	55	52	50	48	45	43	40	38	36	33	31	29
41	98	95	93	90	88	85	83	80	78	75	73	71	68	66	63	61	59	56	54	51	49	46	44	41	39	37	34	32	29	27
40	98	95	93	90	88	85	83	80	78	75	73	70	68	65	63	60	58	55	53	50	48	45	43	40	38	35	33	30	28	25
39	97	95	92	90	87	85	82	79	77	74	72	69	67	64	62	59	56	54	51	49	46	44	41	38	36	33	31	28	26	23
38	97	95	92	89	87	84	82	79	76	74	71	68	66	63	61	58	55	53	50	47	45	42	39	37	34	32	29	26	24	21
37	97	95	92	89	86	84	81	78	76	73	70	68	65	62	59	57	54	51	49	46	43	41	38	35	32	30	27	24	22	19
36	97	94	92	89	86	83	81	78	75	72	69	67	64	61	58	56	53	50	47	44	42	39	36	33	31	28	25	22	19	17
35	97	94	91	89	86	83	80	77	74	71	69	66	63	60	57	54	51	49	46	43	40	37	34	31	29	26	23	20	17	14
34	97	94	91	88	85	82	79	76	74	71	68	65	62	59	56	53	50	47	44	41	38	35	32	39	26	24	21	18	15	12
33	97	94	91	88	85	82	79	76	73	70	67	64	61	58	55	52	48	45	42	39	36	33	30	27	24	21	18	15	12	9
32	97	94	91	88	84	81	78	75	72	69	66	63	59	56	53	50	47	44	41	38	34	31	28	25	22	19	16	13	9	6
31	97	94	90	87	84	81	77	74	71	68	65	61	58	55	52	48	45	42	39	35	32	29	26	23	19	16	13	10	6	3
30	97	93	90	87	83	80	77	73	70	67	63	60	57	53	50	47	43	40	37	33	30	27	23	20	17	13	10	7	3	
29	97	93	90	86	83	79	76	72	69	66	62	59	55	52	48	45	41	38	34	31	28	24	21	17	14	10	7	3		
28	96	93	89	86	82	79	75	71	68	64	61	57	54	50	46	43	39	36	32	29	25	21	18	14	11	7	4			
27	96	93	89	85	81	78	74	70	67	63	59	56	52	48	44	41	37	33	30	26	22	19	15	11	7	4				
26	96	92	88	85	81	77	73	69	65	62	58	54	50	46	42	38	35	31	27	23	19	15	12	8	4					
25	96	92	88	84	80	76	72	68	64	60	56	52	48	44	40	36	32	28	24	20	16	12	8	4						
24	96	92	88	83	79	75	71	67	63	58	54	50	46	42	38	33	29	25	21	17	13	8	4							
23	96	91	87	83	78	74	70	65	61	57	52	48	43	39	35	30	26	22	17	13	9	4								
22	95	91	86	82	77	73	68	64	59	55	50	45	41	36	32	27	23	18	14	9	5									
21	95	90	86	81	76	71	67	62	57	52	48	43	38	33	29	24	19	14	10	5										
20	95	90	85	80	75	70	65	60	55	50	45	40	35	30	25	20	15	10	5											
19	95	89	84	79	74	68	63	58	53	47	42	37	32	26	21	16	11	5												
18	94	89	83	78	72	67	61	56	50	44	39	33	28	22	17	11	6													
17	94	88	82	76	71	65	59	53	47	41	35	29	24	19	12	6														
16	94	88	81	75	69	63	56	50	44	38	31	25	19	13	6															
15	93	87	80	73	67	60	53	47	40	33	27	20	13	7																
14	93	86	79	71	64	57	50	43	36	29	21	14	7																	
13	92	85	77	69	62	54	46	38	31	23	15	8																		
12	92	83	75	67	58	50	42	33	25	17	8																			
11	91	82	73	64	55	45	36	27	18	9																				
10	90	80	70	60	50	40	30	20	10																					
9	89	78	67	56	44	36	22	11																						
8	88	75	63	50	38	25	13																							
7	86	71	57	43	29	14																								
6	83	67	50	33	17																									
5	80	60	40	20																										
4	75	50	25																											
3	67	33																												